DATE DUE

AUG 1 7 1999	OCT 2 1 2000
AUG 2 6 1999	JAN 0 5 2001
AUG 3 1 1999	MAR 5 2001
SEP 2 2 1999	APR 0 9 2001
OCT 2 9 1999	APR 1 6 2001
JAN 3 1 2000	MAY 1 6 2001
MAR 1 0 2000	JUL 2 8 2001
MAR 1 1 2000	SEP 2 0 2001
MAR 2 3 2000	DEC 0 7 2001
APR 1 3 2000	SEP 2 7 2002
MAY 0 9 2000	NOV 0 6 2002
JUN 1 5 2000	APR 2 5 2006
	JUN 0 7 2006
JUL 1 2000	
JUL 2 4 2000	
AUG 1 5 2000	
SEP 1 5 2000	
SEP 2 6 2000	

GAYLORD

PRINTED IN U.S.A.

Nightingale's
Adventure
in Alphabet Town

by Laura Alden
illustrated by Jodie McCallum

created by Wing Park Publishers

CP CHILDRENS PRESS ®
CHICAGO

Library of Congress Cataloging-in-Publication Data

Alden, Laura, 1955-
    Nightingale's adventure in Alphabet Town / by Laura Alden ;
illustrated by Jodie McCallum.
        p.   cm. — (Read around Alphabet Town)
    Summary: While collecting sticks to build a nest, Nightin-
gale is hit on the neck by a nut and is taken to the hospital by
his friend Nellie the nurse. Includes alphabet activities.
    ISBN 0-516-05414-7
    [1. Alphabet.   2. Nightingales—Fiction.]   I. McCallum, Jodie,
ill.   II. Title.   III. Series.
PZ7.A3586Ni   1992
[E]—dc 20   92-1069
                                                              CIP
                                                               AC

Nightingale's
Adventure
in Alphabet Town

You are now entering Alphabet Town,
With houses from "A" to "Z."
I'm going on an "N" adventure today,
So come along with me.

This is the "N" house of Alphabet Town. Nightingale lives here.

Nightingale likes everything that begins with the letter "n."

That is why Nightingale always wears a

necktie.

And why he likes to write

Nightingale also builds

nests

for other birds.

He sells them for a nickel each.

One day when Nightingale was looking for sticks for a new nest,

a nut

fell on his neck!

Oh, no! Poor Nightingale.

Nightingale's neck hurt. He needed
help. But no one was near him.
"Help, help!" he chirped.

Then Nightingale heard a noise. It was his friend, Nellie the nurse!

15

"I am so glad to see you," said Nightingale. "A nut fell on my neck."

Nellie looked at Nightingale's neck.
"Your neck will soon be as good as
new," said Nellie.

Nellie took Nightingale to the hospital.

She put a

nightcap

and nightshirt

on him.

A doctor named Ned came to see
Nightingale. "Your neck will be
fine," said Ned. "But you need to
rest."

"Take a nap now," said Nellie to Nightingale. "I will take care of you."

Nellie never left Nightingale alone.
She kept his room nice and neat.

Nightingale stayed in the hospital
for nine days and nine nights.

23

Nightingale's neck felt much better.
"Now you can go home," said Nellie
the nurse.

So Nightingale took off his nightshirt and his nightcap.

"Thank you for taking care of me," said Nightingale. "Here is a gift for you."

"A necklace!"

said Nellie. "How nice."

Then Nightingale said good-bye
and went home.

And the next day, Nightingale
went back to building nests.
But he watched for falling nuts!

MORE FUN WITH NIGHTINGALE

What's in a Name?

In my "n" adventure, you read many "n" words. My name begins with an "N." Many of my friends' names begin with "N" too. Here are a few.

HELLO my name is Nina	HELLO my name is Nick	HELLO my name is Nancy

HELLO my name is Nicole	HELLO my name is Ned

HELLO my name is Nate	HELLO my name is Norm	HELLO my name is Nora

Do you know other names that start with "N"?
Does your name start with "N"?

Nightingale's Word Hunt

I like to hunt for "n" words. Can you help me find the words on this page that begin with "n"? How many are there? Can you read them?

nails

candle

pen

nose

window

kitten

camera

Can you find any words with "n" in the middle?
Can you find any with "n" at the end?
Can you find a word with no "n"?

Nightingale's Favorite Things

"N" is my favorite letter. I love
"n" things. Can you guess why?
You can find some of my favorite
"n" things in my house on page 7.
How many "n" things can you
find there? Can you think of
more "n" things?

Now you make up an "n" adventure.